SO,
YOU WANT TO GET A HORSE?

THE ULTIMATE GUIDE TO ENTERING THE HORSE WORLD

Verena Bowyer

Copyright © 2021 by Verena Bowyer

www.girlabouttheyard.com

Published by Verena Bowyer

ISBN: 979-847-025-957-8

CONTENTS

PART THREE

YOU AND YOUR HORSE

INTRODUCTION

There is an unspoken rule in the horse industry that asking questions is both brave and bold. It is also the simplest way of finding out the information we need; however, there are not enough hours in the day, or minutes within an hour, to ask the questions we have. When starting out at a new hobby, I dive in headfirst and then work out how to learn from there; others, I have noticed, in my time as a riding instructor, have wanted more information before they dive in.

So, this guide is to help you, to provide you with the answers you hadn't realised you needed and to help you navigate the wide equestrian industry with confidence, with clarity and knowing your own mind.

I am Verena, I have loved horses, ridden horses, and cared for horses over the last 20 years and more. I dreamt of being a riding instructor from a young age, as I wanted to bring a voice to the horse world that hadn't been provided before – that I haven't seen in the recent generation – permission to fail and bounce back. I have failed and relearned to pass my British Horse Society exams, I have put my neck on the line for different approaches to horse loving, from tough love to Parelli horsemanship. I wrote a dissertation on the horse meat scandal back in 2013 and whether having a base price for a horse would reduce the amount of equine welfare cases in the UK. The answer was that we are not yet ready for it, but that's another story.

Growing up around horses, I had the luxury of having friends and parents who I could question until I was blue in the face. I could ask them what each term meant, and I could mess up and still feel supported. Moving my horse to a livery yard and experiencing the judgment and the pressure that was so prevalent made me even more committed to bringing another voice to the party. I want you to know that owning a horse can be fun, the passion can very much be there, and it really is as simple as loving your horse.

The things that you crave and desire are the things that make life that little bit more expensive and that is completely natural.

Being born into a family of 'buy well and buy once', things become well used and well loved. Decisions were made that meant that I couldn't have the newest and prettiest of things, which made life more durable. I am in no way standing on a soap box here, instead saying, if I can do it. So can you.

I was taught at a young age by my parents to strip it back, if something is not working, have a look at the basics and then build on that. The horse is misbehaving, is it having too much food? I am struggling with something; what's really going on here... the list goes on. Simplify it; it is rarely as complicated as the human brain wants to make it.

I went to University to study Equine Management (Business) passing with a strong 2:1; I then went on to fail my British Horse Society exams. I'd ridden all of my life, why would I not have passed automatically? Because the standard is high, the reputation is built up of many generations and it made me a better person. I broke down what I knew, and I went back to square one. Back to learning the basics and the right way to do things. The horse never reads the textbook, but they know a calm and confident owner and the horse behaves accordingly.

One of the biggest compliments someone can give me, is that my animals are calm and relaxed. I expect big things from my animals and when they produce that in the public eye, or in front of the postman; I beam with joy.

My wish for this book is that it would help you to feel that supporting arm behind you, encouraging you to take the leap; to trust your instincts and to keep yourself on the path that you were destined to be on. You might read this book and think, get me out of here. That is OK too; horses are made for specific roles and humans are too; a horse lover might not be one of them. Or you might be getting this book to understand why someone you love loves horses; it takes time; it takes commitment but know that whatever the situation is, the person who can love a wild, turbulent animal every day, can love you even more.

It gives me so much joy to invite you to read on; to lap it up and to learn. Lean into what you trust, what you know and what you are going to learn. Being around horses is a learning curve, there is no quick fix and it's a journey that can give you the greatest of adrenaline rushes and have you in the lowest of the low.

Whatever you choose, know that you're right; you're right to choose that and now run with it!

Happy reading and thank you. Thank you for listening to another voice, to adding to your personal development and if we ever meet, let's have a cup of tea. I'll have an Earl Grey, milk with no sugar, please.

Sometimes, it would appear everyone in the horse world already knows how to do it all. Let me let you into a little secret: we are all muddling along with everything, but sometimes it's helpful to have a good standpoint to start from.

I was fortunate to have lots of people around to question, but this is not the case for everyone, so this short guide to help you get the answers you're looking for. Bearing in mind that there will always be more questions, because that's the joy of learning and the excitement of having a new passion!

Before doing anything, make yourself aware of the facilities and resources around you.

WHY GET INTO HORSES?

There are a vast array of benefits to riding horses or even just being involved in the equestrian world.

Not only do you get to play horses and have a best friend whenever you fancy, you also get to be outside in the fresh air. There are also the physical benefits to your health, using your body to get jobs done and when you're riding the horse itself of course. For example, lifting buckets in and out of stables and carrying hay around will almost certainly make you sweat, and when you're walking to the field, so you are naturally using your core. A cheeky core workout without even realising. Yes please!

Horse riding isn't a solitary activity, either. You'll inevitably end up socialising with your fellow riders, either on a livery yard or at events. This is great for your mental health and wellbeing, as well as handy for getting riding tips or to discuss ways of getting that nasty green mark off your horse's bottom.

Owning a horse or having a slot on the livery yard for tending to your loan pony also makes you stick to a routine. As you potter around, tacking up for your lesson or poo picking, you will notice that your mind wanders and your imagination expands, so it's actually a good exercise in mindfulness.

It goes without saying that horses cannot speak. They can, however, show their thoughts and their emotions through their behaviour, as well as their facial and physical features, so when you are dealing with a horse, you are forced to become aware of your own physical behaviour and body language.

Getting involved with horses can help with confidence-building, as horses need the rider or handler to be assertive and clear with their instructions. Riding horses, putting yourself on a wild animal that has its own mind and brain, requires a lot of trust. Trust that the horse will be kind and trust that the human can communicate and keep the horse safe. A confident partnership can change worlds.

If you decide to dive into the horse world, be ready to be passionate in a way you never knew before – and get used to having your time split between "human life" and "horse life".

This is the beginning of something marvellous for you and it's a blessing for me to be able to come alongside you and give you the diving board to jump in at the deep end.

Now, let's get started!

This is the beginning of something marvellous for you and it's a blessing for me to be able to come alongside you and give you the diving board to jump in the deep end.

JARGON

The terminology that is used within the horse world can be quite exclusive, and can make the whole sport inaccessible, as it can be hard to know what people are trying to say. So before we begin, I must demystify things a bit and explain some of the language and common phrases that you might be a bit stumped by. Don't worry – soon they will become your second language!

Aids	term for horse logical pressures – hands (with reins), legs, seat (weight in saddle), i.e., *'Use your aids for your dressage moves', 'be clear with your aid when riding him'*
Bridle	a term for the piece of equipment that is used to direct a horse, i.e. *'I have two bridles', 'my bridle needs a good clean'*
Bit	a term for the components that control and contacts the horse's mouth I.e., *I have so many bits in my cupboard' 'oh I use one bit on my horse'*
Breaking In/Backing	Getting a horse used to the saddle and having someone on their back. This process can be dangerous and should only be done by – or supervised by –

	someone with experience. i.e., *'I sent him away to be broken in, I didn't want to mess it up'*; *'Oh I love backing, seeing the horses relax with you is so rewarding'*
Cavaletti	A jump made of a pole leaning on two X-shaped ends. Can be used for core workouts and as a cross-country jump. Not usually higher than 90cm. i.e. *'I loved cavalettis when I was growing up'*; *'Have you added cavalettis to your schooling? It can do the world of good'*
Chestnut mare	A horse that has a dreadful reputation for being hormonal. i.e., *'Oh golly, she has a chestnut mare'*; *'Honestly; she's behaving like a chestnut mare'*
Clipping	The act of cutting the horse's hair, to allow them to stay cooler and not be sweaty in the winter. This is only necessary if the horse is old and cannot regulate their own temperature or if they're in hard work. Clipped horses must be rugged. *'I am not going to clip my horse this winter, he will have the winter off'*; *'I love clipping, it's so cathartic'*

Colt	A young male horse
Contact	the term to describe the straight line the reins make when they're stretched between a bit and hands, with no loops, i.e., *'pick up your contact, you could hang your washing there', 'my horse does not like accepting the contact on the right rein'*
Cribbing	When a horse bites onto something and pulls back, using their neck to suck in air. Can be considered a stress reliever. It creates this grunt noise that you can hear when you're nearby. Seen as a bad habit. *'Ah, he does crib, do you mind?'; 'My horse has started crib biting when their stable pal is turned out without her'*
Engaged or **engagement**	a term to describe the bending of the horse's hock joints, enabling them to shift his weight from his forehand and carry more weight behind, i.e., *my horse's engagement was amazing, I felt like we were flying' 'I feel a horse engagement really proves they're comfortable.*
Equestrian	a rider on horseback or to something related to horse riding, i.e., *my friend*

	is an equestrian'; 'I couldn't' hack the equestrian world'
Filly	A young female horse
Frog	The triangular part of the hoof that acts as a protective layer for the digital cushion above it. It aids circulation to the hoof and, when the hoof is in action, it acts as a shock absorber. It can be very sensitive, so treat it with care. _'Yesterday, my horse had a stone wedged by the frog, poor thing'; 'I like a healthy-looking frog'_
Gait	the different increases in speed – walk, trot, canter, gallop i.e., _'I love galloping on my horse', 'my horse is most comfortable in trot'_
Gamgee	A highly absorbent and soft padding developed of cotton wool and gauze to create structure and protection for wounds and cuts. _'I've been given some gamgee for my horse's leg'; 'Apply the Vaseline to the gamgee to keep the Vaseline in the right place'_
Green	When a horse is lacking confidence. This is usually down to age but can be due to having little experience. i.e.,

	'He was green in the show jumping ring today'; *'Forgive her, she is green at the moment'*
Hack	Going for a stroll outside of a confided space with your horse, i.e. *'Let's go for a hack'*; *'Oh I love hacking, my horse does too'*
Hair Pulling	When you smarten up the mane or tail by pulling hair out quickly and sharply to keep it tidy. This is usually done after the horse has been ridden so the pores are open. *'I am mane pulling today'*; *'Oh I don't pull my horse's tail; I like the bushy look'*
Halt	coming to a standstill on your horse; aiming for a square halt – hooves in a square formation, in a competition, i.e., *'oh, I got a 5 for my halt today'* *'my horse will stand still in halt for ages'*
Half Halt	Bringing your horse to a near stop, to help them steady and rebalance. *'Half halt at A'*; *'I completely forgot to half halt and my trot became unbalanced'*
Hands (hh)	A unit of 10cm (4 inch) used to measure the horse. *'my horse is 15.2'*

	Horses are anything above 14.2hh, ponies are anything below.
Jodhpurs	Trousers that a rider will wear. They're fitted to the body and are usually navy, grey or white. They're also known as breeches. They have protection on the legs to avoid the rider getting pinched by the stirrup leathers against saddle. i.e., *'I bought some new jodhpurs today, they're so comfy'; 'Did you see those jodhpurs with the fun pockets; quirky!'*
Livery	A term used to describe that a horse is not living at home; it's a service provided by a yard. There are different types of livery, determined by price and what's on offer, i.e., *'is your horse still on livery?' 'full livery only for this week actually'*
Lunging	A form of exercising a horse, where they are on a 20m circle around you and attached to a rope. This works well if you need to see how they're moving or if the rider is looking to perfect their balance. i.e., *'My horse's routine includes one lunging session*

	a month'; 'Oh; I lunged him today, he was naughty!'
Napping	When a horse refuses to go forwards – for example from a yard, from a certain point in the ride, or from mates in the arena. It can be really unnerving for the rider and can start as a result of fear and then end up becoming a habit. *'I cannot stand the napping; it really annoys me'; 'I have stopped my horse's napping by leading him past the "scary" bit'*
Numnah	A pad that goes under the saddle, of a similar shape to the saddle. Also known as a saddle pad. i.e., *'My sponsor is putting their logo on my numnah'; 'I prefer the look of the numnah; it's more subtle!'*
Outline/On the bit	A term to describe a horse's posture relative to the reins and the bridle bit. A position on the bit is submissive to the rider's rein aids, given through the bit. If above the bit, then the head is too high, i.e., *the hardest thing for me is to get my horse in an outline, he prefers being a happy hacker'; 'when*

	a horse is on a correct outline, it really is magical to watch'
Overridden	The act of riding your horse too much; no days off; trying to jump too much or over phasing them. *'Eek, I must give my horse a week off, he's feeling a bit overridden and bored at the moment'; 'It should be illegal to override your horse, they're not robots'*
Pony patter	A nickname for someone that has a horse, implying that all they do is pat their pony. i.e., *'Ha! They're such a pony patter'; 'I love pony patting'*
Quidding	When a horse drops parts of the food out due to bad teeth and being unable to close their mouth. i.e., *'I had a horse that was quidding once, it was very old'; 'Oh, is your horse quidding? I've found chewed bits of food on the floor'*
Ratcatcher	A tweed jacket worn by the hunting field before the hunting season starts on 1st November. Traditionally it would be paired with a boiler hat. i.e., *'It is ratcatcher season'; 'I have misplaced my ratcatcher'*

Roughing Off	When a fit horse is made ready to be turned to grass for a holiday or rest. i.e., *'I have competed all season, I always rough off my horses from October to December'; 'I never see the point of roughing off, but maybe that's because I don't go too hard on my horse'*
Schooling	A bit like going to the gym for a person, this is where you concentrate on achieving something in your riding, i.e. *'I am going to school today'; 'In my schooling today, I managed to do rising trot'*
Self-Carriage	The way that the horse carries themselves, when their body is fully engaged. i.e., *'when my horse carries himself, it floats around the field'; 'Oh, self-carriage is something I strive for in every ride, hack or schooling'*
Sheath	A large fold of skin that protects the horse's penis when it is not extruded for urination.
Sheath Cleaning	The act of cleaning a horse's penis and the large fold of skin protecting it. Grease and grit get in and most are

	self-cleaning, however some horses' penises need a little extra help. This needs to be treated with caution as they are very sensitive. *'Fortunately, I've never had to clean a sheath before'; 'Cleaning the horse's sheath needs to be done carefully. Poor thing!'*
Stable vs Show names	A show name is what the horse has on their passport. This can be a stamp of their breeding or simply chosen by the owner when they were born. A stable name is their 'at home name' or 'nickname', usually much shorter than the show name. The show name is normally said over the Tannoy at an event. i.e., *'I love Frank's show name, How Do You Take Your Tea'; 'That's a fun one, mine is related to where he was born: Evolution Paris'*
Tack up	Putting the saddle and bridle on the horse, i.e. *'I am tacking up my horse'; 'Please could you tack him up for me'*
Turning away	When a youngster gets put out in a field to grow and mature in both character and physical strength. i.e., *'My youngster has been turned away,*

	he's coming back in next week to be broken'; 'Tell me you're turning him away to grow a little'
Turn out	A phrase to describe a horse having a field to live in, i.e., *'mine has all year round turn out'; 'oh I have to pay extra for turn out'*
Turn out (competition)	A competition, or class, where horse and rider are marked out of 10 on their appearance, cleanliness and condition. *'My plaits got a 4 in the tack and turn out, oops'. 'Don't forget your hairnet for the turnout competition'*
Working over their back	When the horse's muscles are working across their back rather than simply moving their legs. The horse is more subtle for the rider and makes a prettier shape. Like a human using their abs to move rather than simply using their back and legs. *'When he works over his back, it's like I'm riding a cloud'; 'I really struggle to get him working over his back while we're hacking'*

Equipment Jargon

Spade	a flat headed tool that cuts in the ground or grass. Good for planting out or cutting edges of grass
Shovel	a flat headed scoop on a pole – good for collecting up piles of muck or mucking out a stable
Fork	a three-pronged tool that works well for lifting soil
Shavings Fork	a tight row of prongs that help collect poo but allow shavings to fall out – usually come in plastic or metal
Pitch-fork	a two-pronged tool that works well for spreading fresh straw and aerating a muckheap
Wheelbarrow	a bucket on wheels that can be filled and transported to another location – these come in one wheel, two wheeled or four wheeled base.
Witch's Broom	a broom made out of stiff fibres, like bristles. A tool good for sweeping dry material. Better in smaller intricate spaces.
Brush	a broom usually made of wood or plastic, that works well for sweeping

away dry or wet material, better for
big spaces.

Part One

Horse-Owning Options

Owning a horse is a big commitment.

The hardest time for a horse owner is deep in the winter, when it hasn't stopped raining and you and your horse are bored. Or when your horse goes lame in the middle of the eventing season.

For this reason, before you jump in to owning a horse, you have to make sure your commitment level is more than simply 'this will be fun' – it needs to be a 'I am committed regardless'. Remember, you still need to put your horse out on Christmas Day. (Though there is something wonderful about popping out to bring your horse in and feed him then, when you're full of food and ready to dive into more chocolate!). There are plenty of other options if full ownership is not possible.

It goes without saying that it is risky to buy a horse without knowing some key points about the horse world, and this goes for sharing too; before you dive in and take on the horse, get some lessons at the local riding school and make sure that you're savvy as to what you're expecting and wanting before anything!

Horses are not an innocent hobby, they need care all year round and cannot be put into a garage at the end of the summer, like a bike.

FULL OWNERSHIP

The all-inclusive, all-responsible option is to own your horse outright. You are responsible for everything to do with it – his worming, his shoeing, his health and welfare – and you have the freedom to do whatever you would like to do with him. He is your responsibility and cannot be put into a garage at the end of the summer.

This is the natural and more common route to horse ownership; however, this requires a huge financial and time investment. This might not suit you if you are strapped for cash or you feel that you don't have enough time to be completely committed. This is not shameful or to be looked at with guilt; being honest about what you can do for the horse is key. Being overwhelmed before you begin will not help the partnership to blossom.

That said, the relationship can change all the time – you might start out as a full-time owner and decide that you cannot sell your horse so you put them on loan or find a friend who would like to share the responsibility and horse share.

As a family or as a parent, owning a horse is a massive commitment too; there is little time or space to do ballet or rugby once you have the horse with you. However, sharing or loaning a horse can give you more options as to how much investment you might make.

Whatever you decide, be sure to keep your priorities and mental peace at the forefront of your mind.

If you've decided to buy a horse, there are some things to consider:

Price

Buying a horse is one of life's real luxuries and can happen on any budget if you are savvy. Costs are entirely measurable and the happiness that you can have with the right horse will outweigh any doubts you have once you meet them.

First off, however, you need to work out what your budget is – you can get horses for any price these days. Start by having a look at the websites in the resources' section of this guide. Prices range massively and are different all over the country. There is no standard going rate. Horses can be priced as a result of the emotional value for the seller, if they are trying to buy something else and need the money for it, or if they want to sell quickly. Prices may also vary depending on what the horse can and cannot do. If, for example, they cannot jump, they'll be cheaper. This is natural but something to be aware of, as you don't want to be caught out with a dud horse simply due to not looking at why it was priced as it was. There are some horses that are complete gems that are sold for a cheap price simply because the seller is realistic.

Price does not dictate how good the horse will be, or how suitable they will be for your job. You could buy a £2,000 racehorse, but he will never be able to pull the cart that you're dreaming of. Just because the price is good doesn't mean the horse will suit you. Similarly, the horse might have a dreadful habit that you cannot stand but be within your budget. Don't be swayed. You will regret it when you're having a down day, so be careful to choose what you really want.

When considering your budget, make sure you have accounted for tack fitting, vetting and travel arrangements. It's also a good idea to get an insurance quote for any horse you're interested in, as costs can vary from horse to horse.

Where to look

Most horses are sold through adverts; if the horse is available for loan, it will clearly state this alongside the price for buying. 'POA' on an advert means 'price on application'. This can be frustrating as a buyer, because you cannot make a decision without speaking to someone; as a seller, however, it is useful, because it separates the time wasters from those really wanting to buy a horse.

Adverts can be found online, in newspapers and in horse magazines. Usually, the advert will contain the size of the horse, the breed and the gender. This helps to narrow down what you're looking for. If you don't like mares, for example, you can skip over these adverts.

Private sales vs. dealers

Horses can be sold in a similar manner to cars: through private sales (non-commercial person to non-commercial person) or by dealers. People use dealers if they don't want the upheaval of showing people their horse or if they haven't found anyone to buy it.

Dealers buy and sell horses for a living. Some don't have good reputations – for example, for not selling the same horse as described in the advert. Be wise to how you feel about the person who is selling. There is nothing wrong in saying 'no thank you' after hearing and seeing the horse.

Bear in mind that some horses go to yards to be sold and may not have been there long enough to show all their quirks. Always ask to speak to the previous owner if possible. If they don't give you their number, leave the advert there. It's not worth the risk.

Viewing the horse

Always view a horse. Never buy a horse without riding and checking them out in person. There are lots of things that a quick edit of a film or photo can remove. Some people have been to see horses that look angelic on the advert and have run at them in the stable when they visited. It's only wise to have a visit before you pay.

There's no doubt about it, the experience of viewing a horse is a bizarre one. Never in your life before or since will you have to make such big, bold assessments of a horse in such a quick time frame. You will be thinking things like: Could I put my granny on this? Would I trust someone to put it out for me if I were to have broken my leg? How much time can I realistically spend with this horse to keep them relaxed? Are they going to be too docile for me? In fifteen years' time, will I remember the joys of what I've enjoyed, or will I be terrified? Would I let my dog off around this horse? When I have the photoshoot of my dreams, will my eye gravitate to one part of this horse's physique? Do I trust the seller? All the while, the owner is trying to tell you about how marvellous the horse is. It is both an empowering and a terrifying experience, and one that you will never forget – indeed, it could change your life forever!

Only a fool would enter into buying a horse without actually riding and becoming comfortable with one beforehand.

Viewing a horse normally takes a couple of hours, during which you will want to see the horse being ridden by someone else. If the seller cannot get on because they have a bad back, go back another time. Horses behave differently when ridden by different people.

Here are some questions you might want to ask the seller at a viewing, in no particular order:

- Why are you selling/putting them on loan/wanting to share?
- What would you say your horse's personality is like? Can you describe them as a human? (This may sound wishy-washy, but if you're not keen on a certain personality – troublemaker, keeps you up at night, etc. – then this can be a good thing to know!)
- Do they have any stable habits?
- How are they with traffic?
- Do they mind having a day off?
- What is your usual weekly routine with them?

Some questions may not be applicable now but allow you to consider the bigger picture. For example, you may not be interested in hacking now, but you should still ask the traffic question, as it would be tricky to have a horse that doesn't like hacking if you end up leaving your livery yard to move your horse home, and then never being able to go anywhere because of the road next door.

As with everything, there are sellers that will give you all the details without much questioning. They are usually private sellers and know the horse very well; this is helpful as they tell you all the quirks and with honesty, which helps you decide if you do, in fact, need the horse that doesn't like to be mucked out by men, for example.

Honest and thoughtful sellers will let you know what's going on behind the scenes, because they would want to know themselves. This is not a discredit to the horse at all; as with animals and humans; there are good and bad sides. It is then up to you to decide what you have on your 'must have' list (see below) and if the horse fits with it.

And remember communication and clarification are key; if you don't understand what someone is trying to say, ask them to explain it a bit further. You are finding a horse that you will enjoy and build a partnership with – the less opportunities for surprises, the better.

Write it down

There are blank pages at the back of this guide for this exact purpose!

There may be things that you cannot stand with horses. You may not want a black and white one, say, or a mare. You might also have strong opinions about the horse having a kind eye but not care about how big their ears are. You might don't not want to travel the length and breadth of the country for the horse. Now write a list of your 'I will not budge' requirements in a horse and your

'luxuries' in a horse. Loaning, sharing or buying outright –
you will still need the list.

Keep the list with you when you're browsing adverts or
talking to people in the industry. It can be handy to keep it
on your phone or in your diary. Being very clear on what
you're looking for and what your non negotiables are, can
help with the success of finding the right now. Don't be
afraid to move around with what you hope for, but having
clear starting points helps.

Compatibility

There is a saying in the horse world – horses for courses.
You do not want to end up getting a horse that hates girls
for your daughter; similarly, you don't want a horse that
doesn't enjoy rain when it will be living in the wettest part
of the country.

You'll likely have to view several horses (the average, in
my experience, is around five) before you find the horse of
your dreams. You may decide that you love the horse but
cannot imagine yourself being able to keep them to the
manner to which they're accustomed. If so, you need to
find another horse.

In the process of finding a horse, you might discover
things about yourself that you didn't realise. For example,
you may think you want a youngster who you can teach, or
a horse you can learn together with. However, if you feel
underconfident with your jumping skill or you're not a

bold person on the ground, a youngster is maybe not the one for you as it's hard to correct both the human and the horse at the same time.

If you are spending a lot of time trying out new horses, use each ride to try your riding techniques; are you better at sitting trot on this one? Why? Is this horse a bit too wild for your granny who might ride later in the year? Would you happily go for a ride in the wind with this horse? Riding different horses enhances your riding skills – all horses are different, and all horses have their positives and negatives!

Be wary of adverts

Naturally, you wouldn't write an advert that reads 'slightly mad horse, cannot walk down the road without spooking but is great fun when you go jumping', so it is wise to look at what is not said in the advert. If it says the horse is good to shoe and tack up, for example, ask whether the horse is okay to load into a box, or good around children.

You may decide you need a schoolmaster – a horse that has a good history of doing everything already. Now, if you read an advert that sounds perfect, but the horse is four years old, they are unlikely to be an actual schoolmaster with only four years under their belt.

If you're reading an advert and falling in love with the horse but it is over fifteen years old, this is not always the end of the world. It would be a good idea to find out about its arthritis experience at that age though, as any aged horse can get arthritis. A bit like a car, look at the mileage of the horse, if it is a fifteen-year-old but has been in a field most of the time, it is going to have a lot more left in the tank than one who has been driving up the motorway towing a trailer every day, so to speak.

Another thing to look out for is if they mention that the horse is competent at hacking, but they don't say if that is on its own or in a group. Ask the question. There may be a reason why something is not included, and you will be able to hear that when you ask the seller the question. For this reason, telephone conversations or, even better, face-to-face meetings are far preferable to emails or messages.

That said, it is a skill to write a good advert, so try not to dismiss adverts that aren't too brilliant, because the horse may be much better than the owner gives it credit for. A bad advert does not always mean the horse is bad. However, stick to your requirements – and use your eyes. If you like the look of the horse in the photo, keep it as an option; if you don't, move on.

Word of mouth

Word of mouth is the most reputable way of buying a horse. If you have contacts in a Pony Club or local riding club, ask them to have an ear to the ground about suitable candidates. Always spread the word – you never know who might hear about a horse for sale. At this time, it is wise to state your preferences on breed, ability, age, height, budget and gender. You may get some recommendations on horses that are not suitable for what you wish for but are close. If so, go and look at them anyway. It is a good idea to see a few 'not quite perfect' ones if only so you can be sure that you have the right requirements.

Get a second opinion

If you fancy an extra pair of eyes, take a professional – they may bill you for their time – or someone you trust who could help you. It is wise to take someone who knows you or what you're looking for, so they you can have a second pair of eyes on what you're buying.

Even before the viewing, try to get videos of the horse and send them to people you trust; videos speak a thousand words and can help you know what the horse will look like physically before you see it. You are under no obligation to go ahead and have a viewing or anything after a phone call and video. You know what you want, you know what good looks like and what bad looks like. Stay true to how you feel about the horse and what you know you want. However, if you have decided not to go any further with a horse, it is respectful to let the seller know promptly.

Consider loaning first if possible

The most upsetting thing about buying a horse is that not all sellers can be trusted. If you go ahead and say you're looking for something safe for your dear daughter, they may say their horse is incredibly loyal and loving and would do just the job, only for your daughter to fall off when you try it at the weekend. If you can, get the horse on loan before you buy. This is a try-before-you-buy type of a sale. It is not too much to ask, but it might not be what the seller is offering, so work out if this is essential for you before you buy.

Medical history

Always look at the horse's medical history. For one, you should know how often a vet has had to be called out for the horse. Does the vet practically live here for this horse, or are they simply seen for their routine vaccinations?

It would be frustrating to get your dream horse and only then discover that they're on calmers just so you can get on their back. This isn't uncommon. There are lots of legal drugs that allow horses to be quiet for a particular role. It's sad but the truth.

Another reason for asking how many times a vet has been out for the horse is so you know what you can get insurance cover against. A lot of insurance companies will not insure against previous injuries. If you already know about the leg injury, or the allergic reaction, you will be able to weigh up whether, if it were to happen again, you would be able to afford to own the horse. Bearing in mind that the vet bills may come around again, and you would be responsible for paying them without insurance help.

Check their passports

Always ask to see the horse's passport before you share, buy or loan. You don't know what has happened before and some horses have been passed across the border on the wrong passports. Don't be a victim of a lie.

Horses for courses

Horses are very much defined by the job that they have. They should not be expected to do something that they physically cannot do. Horses that are forced to be something that they are not will end up unhappy and unwilling to do their job. Be aware of what you're asking for and get a horse breed suitable for that. For example, racehorses do not pull traps well, but a cob would.

Different breeds will be good for different jobs, but also look at their breeding – some horses will be bred for jumping but are not a standard jumping breed as such. Their history will help you to determine what they will be good at. That said, not every horse has breeding that can be recognised, so it is not essential for a horse to have good breeding to be a good horse.

With the breeding choice, be sure to look at where you will be keeping your horse. If it is on a windy hill, go for a hardier breed; similarly, if you are on different terrains a lot, then you will need a breed that is likely to know where its feet are. For example, a more solid breed – the cob, for example – would work well on the side of a hill. The thoroughbred requires more attention, so would need to be in a more sheltered area. This is not saying they would not be able to take the weather, but they are less physically hardy.

Check any extras

If the horse comes with 'tack included', make sure you don't take the seller's word for it. They may have thrown other tack in that they don't want anymore, and it may not fit. Or it was the horse's tack, and it doesn't fit for what you need. Remember, getting a professional to check something over will be an upfront cost but worth it in the long run. As the saying goes: buy well, you buy once.

Dealing with the seller

Some people have gone to see horses and the owners have broken down in tears about how wonderful the horse is, how they cannot face saying goodbye, but they also cannot afford to keep the horse in a good condition anymore. Selling a horse can be nerve wracking, as you never know where your beloved friend is going to end up.

For this reason, and others, it's important to be respectful when viewing a horse; it is not your place to say what's wrong with the horse or make sweeping judgements, as you don't know what is going on behind the scenes. Horses can be for sale for any reason under the sun, and some – for example, because the owner is paying for their messy divorce – are none of your business. It is a good idea to

Whoever is selling the horse does not demote the horse's worth; the horse is still an animal and could be your dream horse.

check why they're selling though – just do so tactfully. When you get back to the seller to give them a yes or no, be ready in case they say that the horse has been 'sold under your nose', which means that it's already been sold to someone else. Some buyers will arrive with cash and a trailer and take the horse there and then. You cannot do anything about this – it is simply par for the course.

Similarly, if you find yourself unable to decide, avoid going back again and again for additional viewings. It is tedious for the seller and can make them sour. If you are very keen, let them know when you're leaving the viewing and find out how many other viewings they have got lined up.

If you're saying yes

Be clear whether you're saying, "yes subject to vetting", or "yes whatever".

Get in contact as soon as you've made the decision and make a sensible offer. For example, if they are asking for £100, offer anything between £70 and £75, knowing that, should the seller not budge, you can go up to £100.

Book the vet into to do the vetting (see below) as soon as you can; the next day is ideal but up to a week can be acceptable. Organise travel as quickly as you can and get your horse to you.

If you are unable to receive the horse right away, you may find that the seller will rent you the stable the horse is in until they come to you. Most sellers are flexible, but if it is someone's business, they will want to refill the stable as soon as possible. So, be speedy but safe.

If you're saying no

If you have been to see the horse, take a night to sleep on it and then get back to the owner as soon as you can with your feedback – positive or negative – as to why the horse is or isn't the one of you. Feedback is helpful but be respectful.

Vetting

There are different stages of vetting (information taken from the RVC website):

Stage 1: This is a thorough clinical examination of the horse at rest to detect any apparent signs of injury, disease or physical abnormality. It includes a thorough palpation of all the limbs, listening to the heart and lungs with a stethoscope and an examination of the horse's eyes in a dark stable with an ophthalmoscope.

Stage 2: Observation of the horse walking and trotting in hand in a straight line on a hard, level surface, including flexion tests. The horse is normally also trotted on a small diameter circle on a firm surface to detect subtle lameness issues.

Stage 3: Observation of the horse performing strenuous exercise, normally under saddle. This allows further evaluation of the way the horse moves and assessment of the heart and respiratory systems' response to exertion. If ridden exercise is not possible (e.g., if the horse is unbroken), this stage may be conducted by exercising the horse on the lunge.

Stage 4: A period of rest in the stable to give time for any stiffness induced by the exercise to become apparent. During this time the respiratory and cardiovascular systems are monitored as they return to their resting levels. The horse's markings are normally recorded, and the passport examined.

Stage 5: A second examination of the horse at trot in hand. This is primarily to check that the strenuous exercise has not exacerbated a subtle underlying lameness problem. Flexion tests or trotting on a small diameter circle are sometimes repeated at this time.

The most common stages used are stages two and five, but it all depends on how thorough you wish to be. X rays can also be included for an extra fee.

A vet will come and look at the horse, do an assessment and then report back to you from there. There are vets that will ring you when they arrive on site, then ring when they've seen the horse to report back in raw form, then follow up the call a week later to see what you have decided. There are some vets who will simply give you the report after they've done it. It is recommended to get a vet who isn't already the horse's vet, so they cannot join forces with the seller to be dishonest with you.

Don't lose hope

Buying a horse takes a lot of energy, a lot of mental strength and a lot of general restraint. There are a lot of beautiful horses out there, so be ready to be let down a few times, for you to feel like your heart is being ripped out from underneath you. Keep looking and try to avoid losing hope.

If you are met with multiple options and none that seem to suit, go back to your list of 'could have' and 'non negotiables'. You're thinking about the long-term partnership here, not the next week or next event challenge. Some horses take many years to find, others take a couple of weeks. Allow yourself to be patient. You will find the one you're dreaming of. It might just be a longer process than you had hoped.

The bottom line is finding your perfect horse, and you'll never look back! Jump in early without proper consideration – and you'll struggle to put your wellies on in the morning!

If you feel unable or unwilling to commit to a full ownership or responsibility of caring for the horse, here are some other options. Remember: your horse loves you regardless of what 'ownership' level you're on!

LOANING A HORSE

This is where you are not the legal owner on the horse's passport, but you are in charge of the day-to-day life, the welfare and the exercising. You are effectively owning the horse, but you can give them back should you grow out of this horse through progression up the competition levels or your needs change and the horse becomes unsuitable. The owner will be able to move the horse on to another rider or loaner if this is the case. The owner can also choose to take back the horse should your expectations not meet theirs. It is essential to get a signed agreement of terms of use; you don't want to be left high and dry with your guard down later on.

You may end up loaning a horse for so long that the owner dies or they offer you ownership of the horse for a small rate, less than the standard market cost of the horse at the time. This is a gesture of goodwill, as they may see that you are likely to loan the horse forever and may wish to be the sole and legal owner.

Financially, the cost of loaning a horse can be different for everyone; some people may wish to pay for everything, and the loaner simply asks for more feed, or for the farrier's bill to be paid. This is common in an older owner or someone who is not interested in riding the horse but instead loves the idea of owning and knows that the horse would be happy with a gentle rider.

SHARING

This is where you might take full responsibility for the horse, on three days out of the week, for example. This works well if you or the owner are looking for a horse but are unable to commit to a full ownership timescale due to life commitments. Similarly, you might find this is easier if you travel a lot for work and can only ride at the weekend.

This is cheaper than full livery, as you will have someone to keep the horse loved while you are busy but at no extra cost.

Make sure that you know if you're splitting the bill or if you are responsible for different parts of the financial commitment. As with loaning arrangements, conversations are key. Assumptions are rarely correct.

A loaner or a sharer horse may be able to move yards, or it may be in writing that the horse must stay where they have been based before. Make sure you clarify this with the owner. It would be crazy idea to share a horse in the south of the country, for example, if you live in the north!

With both loaning and sharing, it is crucial that you get a contract, or terms of agreement, drawn up. It's not worth risking otherwise. This should include the answers to the following questions:

- Who pays for feed? Will there be any communications about changes should either party discover a preferred feed combination?
- Who foots the livery bill?
- Who pays for vet bills/farriers/wormers/insurance?
- What happens if tack is broken?
- Who pays for competition entry fees/transport costs?
- How much notice does either party need before they can change the rota?
- Will there be a calendar to mark who is riding or responsible for the horse when?
- How specific is the routine; does the horse struggle with change?
- How are we paying for this?

Be mindful of how much you want to spend each month; it isn't advisable to try to squash more things into your budget to please others, as you will end up being the one having to carry the financial burden.

There may be the option to pay money into a bank account and both have cards on the account to pay for everything. This is a strategic way of sorting out what is in your budget.

Whatever route you decide to go down, get the agreement written in ink. With signatures. People's lives change, and you cannot control that, but you can keep each other accountable through formal agreements.

NON-OWNERSHIP

If you are unable to commit the time and money into owning, sharing or loaning a horse, but would love to ride regularly, keep going to your riding school. There are lots of benefits to this, including:

You get the friend that comes with repeat lessons, and you will grow to know a range of different horses and be a more well-rounded horse rider. (This is a downside to owning or having a financial input into a horse as you end up only really committing to that one horse – unless you buy multiple of course!)

You will be able to get involved with lots of the extra options at the riding school. There may be a horse that you would be able to ride regularly and, in essence and nature, own, but without the financial and time investment.

A riding school will also keep the horse, and the costs included in your lesson cost. This will provide you with a great way of experiencing horse ownership. You may also be able to compete on the horse and be able to get the full experience.

TIP: Make sure that you have tried all the instructors in the school as you may not be able to get external teachers in to help you – this is a strategic decision from the riding school as they know what both the teacher and the horses are like.

The equestrian world is meant to be fun, so choose what will suit you. If you are unable to commit to owning a horse in year one of your journey in the equestrian world, that is OK and totally normal. Year three or four might be your year for full time and financial commitment.

Conversations are key. Assumptions are
rarely correct.

Part Two

The Practicalities of Horse Ownership

STABLING

Your biggest cost will be where you keep your horse. This may be a livery yard, or it may be a field that you rent to house him. Either is normal and it should fit your price range. Skimping on where your horse lives for luxuries will make the long-term enjoyment harder. For example, if you buy a lovely new saddle but cannot keep your horse healthy, the saddle won't fit, rendering you and the horse uncomfortable and unhappy. A happy horse means the luxuries can be used!

There are a few options for livery to choose from:

FULL LIVERY

This will cost the most and will include everything – feed, bedding, turning-out and bringing-in services, changing rugs and anything else you require. Your field will be maintained for you – this is through poo picking, cleaning water troughs, keeping the gateways clear and removing any weeds or poisonous plants. You will also get full use of the facilities. The yard will be at your disposal as you are a higher-rate payer. You may wish to include exercising in this package, depending on your personal preference. For example, if the rider is away at school or lives away and only comes up for the weekend, then it would be wise to get the yard to exercise too, if this is an option. That way the horse is ready to be ridden and fit enough for the standard of work the rider is expecting. The vet and farrier bills may be paid for you and you then pay it off on the invoice all in one go. Worming may also be included in your package.

PART LIVERY

Part livery, also known as "assisted DIY", is what it says on the tin: you do part of the job. This can range from everything apart from riding to only helping out when you're on the yard rota to do so. Part livery normally means that you will do the bulk work and then get help from the yard as and when it suits you.

For example, you may wish to muck out, ride and be at the yard in the morning but may be unable to come down to bring in your horse for the evening routine. You would then get a member of staff to bring your horse in. Included in your part livery will be cleaning water troughs, poo picking and sorting out the field maintenance.

Do check all this with your livery yard, however. Facilities-wise, you may get full access, but you may also need to pay the bills for the bedding, hay, vet and farrier rather than those costs being added to your invoice.

DIY LIVERY

This is the cheapest livery option, and normally it means that you will simply have a stable available to use. You are expected to do both the morning and end-of-the-day routines. You will be expected to maintain your own field, keep your horse happy and be in charge of poo picking and keeping poisonous plants out of the field. Your worming regime, your farrier appointments and any vet calling will need to be done yourself. You are essentially looking after your horse as if it were at your own home but using another person's land and facilities. This is by far the most hands-on option.

The livery yard you are at may offer a service where you can be billed for help at either end of the day. For example, if you cannot get to the yard because of another commitment at the time that the horses have their evening routine, you may be billed say £3 each time you are assisted by the livery yard staff. This is helpful because it takes the weight off your mind but remember to be savvy with your costing and budget. It may be wiser to do part livery if you are using the "bring in service" every day.

AT HOME

Keeping your horse at home might be a dream, it might also fill you with fear. It is a new level of responsibility as there is no one on site to help at short notice. If you are keeping your horse at home, you will need to source your own staff for any days you may be away. You will ultimately be doing the same as you would for DIY livery but from your own yard. As such, you will also be required to source your own bedding, hay and feed merchants. Making sure you know good grassland management will keep your costs down. The books on the resources page of this guide are a good starting point. Don't be put off by this, though – having your horse at home and looking over the stable door at you with no prying eyes is worth its weight in gold and faff!

CHOOSING A LIVERY YARD

Choosing a livery yard can be hard but it doesn't have to be. Here are some things to bear in mind when choosing a livery yard:

Horses should be turned out, one horse per acre.

Stables should be at least 12m x 12m.

Fresh water must be available at all times.

Horses are herd animals so must be able to see each other if they're not in the same field.

Although some noise is fine, horses thrive off quiet spaces.

Looking further than the facilities, look around and ask yourself:

- How tidy are the other horses?
- Does all their equipment match colour wise – known as matchy/matchy?
- Is the yard clean and tidy?
- Do you mind that the horses have water buckets that need refilling rather than automatic water?
- Is it likely to be super muddy in the winter?
- Will you be the only person not competing?
- Will yours be the only horse who's not able to socialise with others?
- Are the stables far apart?
- Does there seem to be a community?

Some of these aspects may seem trivial at the moment, but the small things soon become big things when you're not having a good time. So, look after your future self and nit-pick which yard you choose. Nit picking is not criticising; it is choosing what you want to have and making it a priority. There are plenty of horses out there and there are plenty of livery yards out there too; help yourself and send some time being specific on what you are looking for.

FRIENDSHIP ON THE LIVERY YARD

Some of the best mates are found on the livery yard. It can be a heavenly spot to drink tea and potter around.

You may have read stories about girls all chatting away about their ponies and what colour headcollar they'll buy and use. Well, in real life, I can tell you there is something hilarious about the kinds of conversations that horse people have! We all talk about effectively nothing, but horses also bring people together. It is a small but magical group of people that understand the madness of horses, the unreliability of the machinery – especially just before an event – and the craziness of horse owners to be out in all weather.

THE COSTS OF HORSE RIDING

Horses can cost a lot if you let them.

Work out your budget and then put your costings out of that; there will be equipment and yards that fit with your budget. Be savvy and stay true to what you need to do rather than what is "cool" or others are telling you to do.

You will notice a difference in price where you are in the country too. Research this, because it might be worth keeping your horse over the border if there is a significant price difference.

Bearing in mind what you can afford, maybe a new rug every other year or cutting back on feed to help keep costs down will be a wise way of helping yourself. Marketing around the horse world is incredibly captivating and it is wise to avoid being caught up in it by writing down what you can afford to spend on and what you can't. For example, I have one bridle and move my bits around; I don't have separate dressage and jumping bridles. I don't feel the need for them and, also, I don't want to do that much tack cleaning!

Similarly, I ride and only have one saddle. This is personal choice, and it is right that you fit your needs to your own desires. Having more than one saddle may be higher on your list than other equipment. Writing down your own priorities will help you get clear on this.

Different shops can range in quality and price, so it is clever to get a set of different quotes and then go from there. Remember: asking for a price list does not immediately mean you have to buy from that shop! You might get better haylage at a cheaper price or you may get poorer hay at a more expensive price. It is not unheard of. Remember, if there is a demand, the price can go up. If no one else is looking for the best price in the area, and so takes all the bad hay, the price will rise. That is business, so keep your head on your shoulders and look around.

UNEXPECTED BILLS

Unexpected bills are the biggest threat to your mental peace with your horse and the longevity of your partnership – mainly because if you don't have the money for the essentials, your horse may become a welfare issue. This can be avoided, however, by being strategic with your budgeting (see below).

The most regular unexpected bills are usually the result of an emergency, and this can be avoided by paying for insurance. There are multiple different options to choose from; you can opt for insurance all the way from loss of life to just your vaccinations.

A good idea is to have a bank account just for your horse's expenses; this way you know what you've bought and when.

On this note, putting aside, say, £100 a month can help for insurance instead of paying it out to an insurance company; then, if you don't spend the "emergency" money for over a year, you've saved your £1,200. This doesn't help with massive surgeries, however, so do be clever with your options.

Another question on big surgeries, as horrid as it is to consider, but is there a particular injury or extent of injury that would result in loss of life? Putting your horse to sleep rather than recovering from a fractured limb, for example? Not a comfortable thought, but essential for the budgeting conversation.

Horses are wild animals, which means they do things we don't expect or could never guess would happen.

As a rider, you may find that you are in need of new kit; this is usually planned, unless you fall off and have to have your jodhpurs cut off for instance! A way of managing your costs can be to set yourself yearly "allowances". For example, you have a new jacket every second winter, focusing on water-proofing each winter and keeping your base layers to their thickest and most practical. You may only wear your best boots for actually riding rather than mucking out and bringing the horse in from the field. Smaller costs like new hairnets and riding socks can be sucked up with your usual costings.

In terms of your yard or grass management, repairs can be expensive and sporadic. Say a horse jumps through the fencing; this will be an upfront essential expenditure with no warning. Similarly, if the weather is bad, you may be keeping your horse in the barn with forage for longer than you'd hoped. Should there be a leak in the water pipe that isn't noticed, this could be a hefty bill that wasn't foreseen.

The general approach with costs is to do a regular stock check and keep your kit high quality. Buy well and you buy once. For this, making sure that your hay is the best quality means you won't need to feed as much to keep your horse in good health. Similarly, if your gateways are hard standing – which can be a horrid upfront cost – you can reduce the amount of grass that is pouched and made into mud and keep mud fever at bay for the horses. Assessing rugs on the horse and repairing any tears can reduce further damage. Barbed wire makes more tears than it is worth having, so, if you can, swap this out for plain wire. It still does the job, while keeping the rugs intact!

A NOTE ON RUG USE

There is a tendency to over-rug, and this can be made more likely because the rider feels the cold whereas the horse does not. If the horse is stabled, they should have more rugs due to not being able to move around to keep warm. Horses that are clipped should also be rugged more in general due to having their natural warmth removed.

A tip to help you know if your horse is warm enough, put your hand behind their ears, at the top of their neck; this is like their own thermostat. If it is warm, leave them as they are; too cold, add a layer.

SHOPPING ON A BUDGET

Owning a horse can become even more expensive when you throw in full prices for equipment. The second-hand market in the horse world is a fruitful and useful place to get acquainted with. A lot of people will buy things, then life gets in the way, it turns out they don't use it, or it does not fit, resulting in a discounted rate for some perfectly good equipment.

There are some items of safety that it not recommended that you skimp on or get second-hand. These include riding hats. You need a hat that fits your head perfectly and keeps you safe. They should be fitted correctly and with the right advice from a trained professional. As a hat cannot be dropped more than 10 times before it needs to be replaced, it's wise to not risk it and buy new. The hat provides comfort and safety for the rider; without it, you are not able to compete, in some places not able to ride, and, most of all, you will not have a comfortable time on your horse.

Head to your local tack shop or feed shop and have a look on their notice boards. There will be some good things there, going for cheap. Think about whether any items you already own can be repurposed; do you have a bucket in the house that can be used as a feed bucket, for example? Washing-up liquid works just as well for cleaning tails or legs as expensive shampoos, and regular silver polish gets the best shine on your stirrups out there!

If you are looking at adverts for second-hand kit, remember to check the wording carefully. Some will say "good for parts", which normally means that they are no longer fit for purpose for their original job, so not

recommended to buy for said original job! For example, if a show jacket is "good for parts", it might be a decent jacket with no buttons, or it might have no sleeves but be good for the buttons!

Buying online, through eBay or Facebook, is rather effective. When you search for goods, be that rugs or tack, keep an eye out for why they are selling. If the rug is no longer waterproof, and they're emptying their yard, the rug may not be suitable for you.

Tack can be bought online, but because the saddle directly affects how the horse moves, it must be fitted to your horse. Saddle fitters will come out and do a good job fitting their own saddle or the saddle you provide.

Remember that buying rugs or tack without measuring and checking can be expensive. You may end up with four bits that don't fit your horse and be out of pocket as a result. There are some places online where you can hire tack for a discounted rate and pay if you decide you like it. Similarly, you could always ask a friend if you could borrow their bit and then buy your own once you've decided you want it.

TIP: Check your tack regularly for any weakened stitching and get it mended when you're not needing it – for example, your stirrup leathers may need some new stitching, and this could be done while you are not riding and on holiday, for example. Wipe your tack down after you use it, to allow it dry without cracking. This also provides a good chance for you to notice any weakness.

AT HOME RECIPES

Some items can be made at home and are just as effective as their bought counterparts. Not only are the following recipes good for keeping costs down, but they are also fun to do on a rainy afternoon.

Homemade Coat Shine:

1/4 cup hair conditioner – horse or human
1/4 cup baby oil
2 tablespoons vinegar (to keep flies away; this is optional)
1/4 cup water

Mix and use in a spray bottle. Remember to avoid the part where your saddle goes!

Buy well and you buy once.

Homemade Fly Repellent:

2 cups white vinegar
1 cup Skin-So-Soft oil (original product by Avon)
1 cup water
1 tablespoon eucalyptus oil

Add all ingredients to a spray bottle. Do not spray directly into eyes or nose; instead, spray some repellent on your hand or a cloth and wipe around the horse's eyes and face.

Homemade Mane and Tail Lotion:

2–3 tablespoons regular conditioner (human or horse)
Hot (not boiling) water
Optional: essential oil of your choice

Add ingredients to a spray bottle. Shake well. Spray on mane and tail, leave for 30 seconds and then brush out with a stiff brush.

To sum up, here are some things to consider on costs:

Will you insure your horse, or will you put money aside each month to cover the freak accident, or the kick in the field that has left a flap of skin off your horses' knee? Vet bills can be over £1,000 a go...

Will you insure your tack? What will happen if there is a late-night raid of the tack room or if your car is stolen? Again, will you purchase insurance or put the money aside each month?

If you fall ill, will you have to pay extra in both livery and home care for your horse? How does the winter work when you fancy going away for the month?

If your horse goes lame, will you have to pay extra cover for your horse to be looked after while you're not available?

How much can you save on vet bills by getting the rest of the yard to have their vaccinations on the same day?

Farrier costs increase if you can't find the shoe for the farrier to put back on – would it be worth investing in a metal detector?

What would happen to my horse if I lost my job? Do I need to save a bit more each month to account for that possibility?

If money becomes tight, what would be my first thing to go? The extra food for my horse or the lesson each week?

Would having a group lesson help keep costs down?

Would changing from a lorry – which has separate insurance, road tax and MOT – to a car that tows a trailer make more sense?

Mucking out in short boots or wellies will keep my long boots looking smart for longer; what else can I have a "everyday" and "special occasion" version of?

Part Three

You and Your Horse

BODY LANGUAGE

Horses show you a lot of what they want to say in how they behave with you. For example:

Ears up when you walk into the field – great sign.

A whinny when you come around the corner – true love and the dream.

Less interested in what you're asking them to do than they normally are? What's bothering them? Are they feeling foot sore? Go back to basics and see if you can solve the issue yourself.

Ears back when you go to feed them – "Give me the food quickly!"

How you behave around your horse will also dictate the mood. A happy horse is soft and peaceful around you. An uncomfortable horse can be abrasive to protect themselves. Watch how the horse moves in the field or wherever you are with it and read the language.

Once you get the simple nuances of what the horse is trying to say and how they behave, you will be able to enjoy each other's company in peace and without worry. It is wise to get to know any horse and their behaviour before you venture into doing anything.

The more time you spend around horses, the quicker you will understand their language. The slight tilt of the ears, the soft or intense eyes, the way they move their backside to tell you something. Until you are confident in what you know, it's a good idea to relax and simply watch.

Do they notice you when you are by the stable? Do they look at you when you come to the field? Are they wanting to get near you or far away from you when you put your hand out?

As you walk towards the horse, look up at them with squared shoulders (shoulders back and your chest out). This shows the horse that you mean business and that you are wanting to do something. If you are resting with the horse and you expect them to rest too, you can relax your posture and not stand so tall.

Being aware of your body language will help you to connect to the horse. In the same way that entering a room with a grumpy face doesn't help the mood, entering a stable like that doesn't help either. Horses are very aware of how people walk and move because that's how they show others in their herd how to behave.

The "big cheese/alpha male" in the pack will chase the other smaller males out of the herd if they're being bullies to the females. They will push their bums and their necks into them to get them to move away. You will also spot that a foal and its mother play around, and when it's time to rest or stop playing, the mother will move her neck and push the foal out of the way. The same happens with giraffes.

Knowing what you're doing with your body language will become a natural reflex, but in the beginning, be assertive when you mean assertive and loving when you are wanting to show that you have an attachment to the horse. Hitting a horse is never the answer. Break it down and work out how to communicate what you're asking. They could be timid around men or not like the hole in the fence; choose to be a team with them not a leader and their subject.

Horses are very sensitive, both physically and emotionally; if you notice a horse that is worried, they will look worried in the eye and their body language will be jumpy. Be mindful when you see a horse for the first time how they react to you. Similarly, you can spot a really happy horse from a mile away, as they will be relaxed and enjoying themselves or sleeping!

Horses and ponies are very similar in their reactions, but ponies are hardier. They are more likely to put up with being pushed around – a bit more like a child. It takes less to form long-term damage on a horse, so be mindful when you're around horses.

Horses love to love, whether that's to whinny back or to nuzzle into you; allow them to enter your personal space and make it a happy place. Allow them to know you're a safe space. The bond that you get with your horse when you cross this bridge is what everyone hopes and dreams for.

Be present when you're around your horse. Be aware of how they're reacting to you. They may be super confident one day and ask you to move away the next. These are good ways to see how your horse is dealing with changes in the season or dealing with changes in their routine.

Horses love to have their own personal space and will tell you if they don't like that you're so close. Keep your eye out. If a horse is moving their bum towards you, this is a signal to "please move away from me" – so listen to them!

TIPS FOR THE UNDERCONFIDENT AROUND HORSES:

Extend a bent hand with your knuckles up – a bit like when a lady would give her hand to a man to kiss – and let the horse smell you. They like to smell so they can choose if you're a danger to them or not.

If you're feeding a horse, have your hand flat, fingers together – your fingers will look like carrots if they're folded up or spread out!

Watch the horse's ears. Forward means happy; flat back or pointed backwards means "caution" or "I am not keen". If they're doing this to another horse, this is a sign to get out of the way. If they're doing it to you or another rider, make sure you keep out of the way until they feel more comfortable. If this is happening when you put the saddle on, make sure to get the saddle checked out as they will be sore on their back. This is their way of saying something isn't quite right.

If you're uncomfortable with how close a horse is to you; forcefully push them back with your hand on the horse's neck, mimicking how a horse's mother would do it in the wild.

You will notice your horse licking and chewing when you give them a titbit or carrot, but you may also see this behaviour when you are asking your horse to do something. This means the horse is calculating what you're trying to ask them to do. Be patient and let them have a second to work out what you're trying to say.

When they stick their head up and show their teeth off, this is their way of saying they can smell or taste something that they're not so sure about. A stallion will do this when they've spotted a mare in season, or if there is a new carrot or titbit on the block. There is nothing wrong with this reaction – just allow the horse to keep sniffing and they will eventually stop!

Turning their head to you when you're standing near them is their way of saying hello, so give them an itch or pat on their neck to say hello back. They're welcoming you into their space.

Some horses lift their head up when you're trying to put the bridle on – this can be a habit, but it could also be a sign to say that they are uncomfortable with the bridle or this particular movement. Respect it. If they are unhappy, make sure to check over the tack or get someone else to help you out.

Some horses will rush into a jump when they are not happy. Check the tack and their surroundings if this continues. It may be the riders' position; it may also be that the horse is uncomfortable. It can be a habit rather than pain, if so, get your trainer to help you sort this.

If a horse whinnies at you, this is a sign of true love. They recognise you as their friend and cannot wait to see you. This is normally because they know you'll feed them when you arrive, but still, I would take it as a win!

A NOTE ON ABUSED HORSES

Abuse can happen to horses, and they are very susceptible to it. They can misread a situation, resulting in the handler getting frustrating and lashing out.

Owners who have not taken the time to understand their horse or listened to them can result in the horse being naturally on the defensive – keeping themselves to themselves and struggling to trust and lean on humans for comfort. These horses need to be handled with care and attention; like with a human, time needs to be taken to learn what they're worried about and how they can be helped.

Abused and hurting horses, physically and mentally, are not write-offs. They simply need more time to feel like they can trust humans again.

KNOWING YOUR WORTH AROUND HORSES

Regardless of where you are in your journey, you are worthy of being on this route. If you are just considering a horse, or you've been riding for many years, you are still worthy.

Once a horse rider, always a horse rider. You're one of the team regardless of how regularly you ride, what your gear is like and how much you value others' opinions.

In an industry where people are all on different places in their paths with horses, it is hard to remember that everyone is at square one at some point; repeatedly. If you're riding a horse for the first time, and you've ridden around Badminton, you're still going through the same things that a new rider would be. How do I stop this horse? Do they move when I ask them to? What are their manners like? What is their personality?

No one is going to come over and tell you that you're too inexperienced to ride, so believe in yourself.

You may find yourself on a horse that is not right for you – similar to when you get a job that you're not suited to. This has no bearing on your worth; it's just a question of suitability and compatibility. Learn from the experience – maybe you're too tall for said horse, or you fancy doing more than the horse can do.

Imposter syndrome around horses is massive. You may get it when climbing onto your horse when you are in a group scenario and your horse doesn't want to stand at the mounting block. It may come when you're thinking about

79

going to buy a rug and you have to ask the shop assistant what weight the rug is.

Remember that, the majority of the time, other people are focusing on their own worries; it is a blessing to know that you don't know what's going through their mind. Maybe they're looking at you because they want to know where your boots are from; or they want to know how to get on and you look calm and collected!

Try not to fret over what you cannot control.

Your horse doesn't read the Instagram posts that you do; they don't see the "this is the best way to do X, Y, Z", and they certainly don't care what you're wearing. All they care about is whether you love them, and it's harder trying to do that when you don't like yourself.

Imposter syndrome doesn't belong in your relationship with your horse, so put it to bed. They love you unconditionally with no judgement, so love yourself in the same way!

As we've seen, the horse can sense what mood you are in. If you're not 100% sure you should be around horses that day, do something else. The mentality that you need to enjoy a horse is not difficult but playing with horses when you are not feeling "you" can be dangerous.

Believe in yourself, the way the horse believes in you. Horses are herd animals, so they thrive off having a leader.

Because domestic horses are now not in herds, you are the herd leader. Step into that role and own it! Know your mind, know your worth and know what fun you can have together.

COMPETITION

The horse-owning journey is a rollercoaster, and it's one worth investing time, money and effort in, but make sure that you don't risk your own mental health and peace with the competition side of things. Keeping your own priorities at the forefront of your mind is a sure way to keep yourself safe. Whatever is costing you your full inner peace, is too expensive. You may need to get a new horse, or maybe you need to step back from where you are and write out what you're hoping for again.

As with all sports, there is competition in horse riding. If it is not directly with yourself or your cohorts, it may be around you. This is natural and fun but keep it healthy.

Everyone is at different stages; everyone is on a different journey. Be mindful of your own mental health by allowing others to do well too; congratulate those who win and be sorry and supportive for those who lose. You never know when a cup of a tea and a "well done you" could go a long way.

COMPETITION NERVES

Competitions aren't for everyone and they're not the definition of success with you and your horse. Measuring success should be done through how you feel with your horse and your partnership. It takes time and it takes commitment.

If you do decide to go to competition, you may find that the nerves take over – butterflies on the drive to the event, sweats when you're thinking about how to ride again and needing to go to the loo every five minutes. You are not alone – even Olympians feel the nerves. It is what you do with them that matters.

When you're going to a competition, take your lesson work to your competition, rather than leaving everything behind when you enter the ring. If you're competing in dressage, think of it as the luxury of having an extra set of eyes looking over your riding, giving you a lesson for the price of an entry fee. Bingo!

If you're jumping, channel your inner superpower and ride your lesson advice like no other; remember, you are not defined by seeing jumping strides. You are judged on whether the jumps stay up and if you fall off – so avoid doing that. That said, if you do fall off or the jump falls, remember that it's a work in progress. Like when you walk up the stairs and slip a little or miss a step – it isn't an immediate reaction to think I've failed, I don't deserve this life; instead, you think, better remember next time to look for the step.

Look for the learning curve, look for the tips to help next time. Help yourself out!

CLOUD NINE AND DISAPPOINTMENTS

It doesn't take long to experience the rollercoaster of horse riding; be that as an owner, a rider or a family member or friend. The emotional rollercoaster of horse riding is a very real thing. You can be riding cloud nine and then fall flat back into real life within a second. This can be done with the extremes, of jumping a jump and, on landing, the horse breaks their leg. The euphoria of jumping and the adrenaline rush of the size of the fence is suddenly overshadowed by your horse having to be put to sleep. It does not matter if the horse is yours or not; the sorrow is still present.

On a less extreme measure but still disappointing, the weather dictates a lot of what happens with your horse – it may be too slippery to go around the particular hack you've been pining for, or it may be too hot to walk on the road as the surface is radiating the sunshine. There can be times when the option to ride in the arena is overshadowed when the snow has fallen or a late frost results in it not being safe.

Try to enjoy the journey, enjoy the love, enjoy the hope.

How you deal with your disappointment is key. Throwing your toys out of the pram and being frustrated with your horse is not helpful; neither is taking it personally and feeling like it is all your fault.

Dealing with a horse that has a stop in an arena or struggles to stop napping just in front of the car on the road is hard. It's a bitter pill to swallow and it makes life that little bit more difficult. But think big picture; with the napping horse, how about jumping off and leading them past the car, just this once? They could take confidence from you and your calm persona going past the car and feel like they can do it.

Analyse and analyse – this gets quicker with experience – what you've been doing and how you've been doing it; are you the reason your horse stops at a jump, or brings a pole down?

The hardest thing to do is be able to separate your self-worth from the issue at hand. You and your horse are still worth a heck of a lot even when the horse stops; or when you are unable to go riding due to the weather. How you grow with your horse is bigger than any "meant to be this way" chat. Ultimately, you're the one that gets to hang out with your horse every day, and you're the one who knows the horse best. So, use that to your advantage.

If your horse comes in from the field without a shoe on a day of training that you've been very excited about, there is no one to blame but nature. The same goes if you're trotting around the arena and suddenly notice that your horse is lame. Or the physio says that rehab has not been successful yet and to give it a few more months.

Not having someone to blame is a hard thing to process, or pill to swallow. Why can't it be someone or something's fault? When you can blame it on someone, it feels like it's half the burden, half the sorrow.

How do you deal with the lack of blame? Think longer down the line. Did the bad luck save you from something in the future that would've been worse? Would going to the event you hoped for actually have ended in disaster? Can you put your best foot forward and try to solve the issue with something like a lesson, or a solution?

Feeling like the world is against you is something that you will get used to. But simply remember that the world is not against you; you are simply hitting a wall. A necessary wall.

This could turn into a quotes and motivational board soon; be honest. Dealing with a wild animal and nature is a hard job. It is a rollercoaster, but you're made of the stuff that survives it.

It is hard to say how you will react to the rollercoaster of having a horse, but know that it is normal to struggle, that you're not alone and that if you need a big cry – go ahead. The tissues are optional.

Cloud nine is amazing. You feel like you can always land on your feet, the adrenaline rushes through your body, you're sweating from the fun and there is simply nothing that can stop you feeling fabulous. This will last as long as you let it – as long as you keep drinking in that cloud nine. When the feeling comes, the idea that you could ever feel like this again is inspiring. Bottle that feeling, keep it for the frustrating days; keep it for the day that you feel like the world is ending. The cloud nine feeling is worth its weight in gold, worth every up and down of the rollercoaster.

The power that comes from the ups and downs - the good and the bad – is addictive. You'll find that without knowing what happens next, you're dreaming of the next rollercoaster.

CLUBS AND DISCIPLINES

The equestrian industry has come a long way from horses being used to round up cows and take their rider into town. This still happens but, alongside that, there are lots of different activities you can get involved with as a partnership now.

The Pony Club is a great place to start. Open to members from the ages of 4 to 25, it is a national body whose main aim is to encourage young people to learn and enjoy all kinds of sport connected with horses and riding. There are centres that are affiliated with the Pony Club, so you don't have to own your own horse to be a member. Whether you own, rent or loan, you can take your horse to the regular rallies and games that they host.

A wonderful feature of the Pony Club are their badges. These are awards for different types of skills within the horse world, from plaiting to designing show-jumping courses. You can also do your Pony Club tests, which give you accreditation for your knowledge and understanding in both ridden and theoretical knowledge. Pony Club awards are widely known and respected.

The competitive horse world can be separated into three main disciplines: Dressage, Show Jumping and Eventing. There are lots of options within these, like showing. Dressage is the skill of getting your horse to work with their full body to perform movements in a comfortable and peaceful harmony with their rider. Dressage takes time, effort, and patience. It is a brilliant indicator in how the partnership works well together. Some have been known to called dressage "horse ballet".

Show jumping is jumping over sticks in an enclosed area under a time restraint. You are expected to jump, cleanly, with your horse over a number of jumps in a course and then you are rated out of your time section to see who wins. One pole down is 4 faults; 2 poles down is 8 points; and 3 refusals – where the horse stops in front of the jump – is elimination.

Eventing combines the two aforementioned disciplines with cross-country jumps. The luxury of cross country is that it is fast paced; it requires endurance and a partnership that is confident to cross the country cleanly. There will be several jumps to jump in a particular order and the terrain will include undulating ground, hills, and water too. Some horses love cross country and others hate it!

Choosing what you would like to do discipline-wise is a useful starting point when considering what horse to buy.

An all-rounder is the perfect horse for someone who fancies dropping in and out of everything. You will find that all-rounders are most popular on the horse market, as they are adaptable and able to mix up their skill set. An all-rounder is not constrained to being an allrounder forever; some are able to master different disciplines.

It is all in the mentality of the horse as to whether they can be re-educated for a certain type of riding style. For example, it is quite possible that if you have a horse that is reluctant to do anything other than be in an arena, you will get stuck trying to make them an eventer or endurance horse. Similarly, you may find that a horse that cannot stand being in the arena will struggle becoming a dressage horse!

The power that comes from the ups and downs, the good and the bad – is addictive.

Riding Clubs

If you fancy pottering around with your horse and enjoying the luxury of what is put in front of you, being part of a riding club could be fun. They have all types of activities, from musical rides to fancy dress alongside competing for your club. You will meet lots of like-minded people at a riding club and it's a great community to be part of. They will also hold many different types of speakers so you can be educated as you learn with your cohorts. What's not to love?

You will need your own horse for the activities, but if your club is based at a riding school, the horses will be available as a facility too! Riding clubs, regardless of your standard, are a great place to start getting into new things. Some may even hold testers and trials for different activities.

Google 'riding clubs [insert area] and see what is around.

Useful Resources

There are lots more out there! These are my favourites:

Books: Pony Club Manual of Horsemanship

BHS Manual of Horse Ownership

Magazines:

Horse and Hound

Horse and Rider UK

Your Horse

Pony Magazine (younger readership)

Websites:

horseandhound.co.uk   www.thehorse.com

Your local vet website   www.ponyclub.co.uk

www.britisheventing.com www.britishdressage.co.uk

www.britishshowjumping.co.uk

SOME FINAL WORDS OF ADVICE

The internet should be treated with an element of caution, or a sprinkle of salt, as there is a lot of unsolicited advice which doesn't care about the results or experience of the consumer. It is a useful space, of course, but aim to get advice and tips from accredited experts too. Try the 80/20 rule – get 80% of your advice from an accredited expert and 20% from the internet. There are experts in every part of the horse world. Some have good qualifications and are accredited; some are not.

Be sure to check the qualifications of anyone that you are recommended by word of mouth. Accreditation means insurance; it also gives you someone to report them to, should something go wrong and it's the quality of service that you can expect and experience. Anyone who is working without accreditation can very easily stop replying to your calls and messages and you are up the creek without a paddle and back at square one with your issue. Think twice, check and trust!

Always ask. It may seem like other people around you, in the horse world, know everything. Alas, despite all they say, they may have more life experience and experience around horses, but they won't know everything. For example, no horse lives as long as their owner, therefore everyone has had to get to know a new horse, and no horse is the same. Coming across as confident and knowing all is part of the game, but if you are in need of some help, ask.

There are people out there who thrive off knowing everything, so test them! It's a fun challenge with your friends who claim to know what's going on. Asking a question does not make you weak or mean you are lacking ability. Not asking a question and getting yourself into a pickle isn't worth the long-term damage. If you're asked to ride someone's horse and you don't ask if the girth has been done up, and then promptly fall off, that is months of damage to your pride because you didn't ask the simple question.

Someone who has grown up with horses for extensive periods of time will take in information and regurgitate the information very freely. It will be a foreign concept that someone may not understand what they mean. For example, why wouldn't you know the difference between a mare and foal? To them it's obvious. Some concepts/terms mean different things to different people – be that geographically or on the same yard – so be ready to adapt, ask questions and hear differences in opinions!

On that note, always, always get a second opinion. That can be from a friend or a professional. If you find that you do not agree with what someone is saying, that is OK. You are entitled to listen to advice and not take it. It is sensible to hear two different opinions and decide on that.

Getting to grips with all of the information will take time, and every day is a school day with horses, so lap it up! The industry is complex, but the love is there!

Final Note

Your adventure doesn't start with the horse, it starts when the burning passion arrives. It doesn't end when the horse is no longer a feature in your life, in fact; it is bigger than the horse and the human.

The adventure you go on, regardless of how it ended, was the happily ever after. It had its ups and downs; it had the 'what am I doing' moments and it had the 'why would I do anything else' moments.

Wild horses and humans are meant to be together; it's just now you wish to take the next step. Get yourself in the saddle and let the adventure begin... it is time to start the adventure of your life.

Notes

Notes

Notes

Notes

Notes

Notes

Printed in Great Britain
by Amazon

66562396R00058